Living From a
WHOLE HEART

Healing the Six Wounds of the Heart

PERSONALIZED WOUNDS

6

DEBBIE ADAMS

Published by

Heart of Heaven Ministries
www.heartofheavenministries.com
e-mail: info@heartofheavenministries.com

Cover design by LindaLeeCreates.com

Dedication

This book is dedicated to my father Jim Hart, whom I have affectionately called "Daddy" my whole life. His life and the love he poured into his family, his children, and especially to me, made this book possible. His perseverance through the painful struggles of life taught me what sacrifice looks like. His faithfulness taught me to believe that nothing is impossible if we will stay the course. And his tenderhearted care for our family taught me how love is demonstrated in human form. Words can't adequately convey how much I love him and cherish his influence in my life. But my hope is that this book will add to his reward in heaven—for without him, my life would have most assuredly looked very different than it does today. Enjoy this book, Daddy—it is the fruit of your life, too.

Acknowledgements

My fondest gratitude goes to the ones who have had the greatest impact on my heart over time.

To Mike: Instead of giving up when the road got really rough, you laid down your own life to help ours come alive. Your countless hours of "working the details" in every facet of our lives together have made it possible for me to thrive. Thank you for all of your sacrificial love and commitment to me. Your reward is coming—and it will be with you for all eternity. I love you now and forever.

To Janna: You are my multi-faceted treasure. You've been a warm and loving daughter, bringing life and joy to my heart on days when all I could see were the storms around me. You have been a honing tool God has used to scrape the rough edges off of my own heart as your iron sharpens mine. You are the most precious best friend any mother could ever hope to have in a grown daughter, a beautiful young woman whose life I cherish and am privileged to steward and to know.

To Jeff and Te'Aira: I have been immensely blessed by the consistency of your lives, the steadiness of your journey, and the unwavering love and honor you have shown us, even when you wondered if we had "lost our marbles" to the unconventional crazy turns we've taken over the years. The precious fruit you have given us in little Kayden and Mikea'Lea are joyful reminders of the earlier days of your own childhood, as well as the hope of our future, as you train them to be all God desires them to be. They are the best gifts you could have possibly given to our family. My heart is full when I am with you all!

To my editor, Christina, to my graphic artist, Linda, and to my friends, Jewell, Teresa, Yvonne, Jeanie, Tamara, Melissa, Sherri and Natasha: Without you these books would never have been finished. You've lifted my heart time and time again with your encouragement, your prayers, and your belief in my ability to cross the finish line. You each share in the fruit that will come from this endeavor. Thank you for being such exceptional people and such faithful friends.

Table of Contents

Introduction

For just a minute let's go back in time to 1958 on a little residential street in California named Anna Ave. That was the street I lived on as a very young girl, and in that year I was a five-year-old kindergartener. My parents bought that particular house on Anna Avenue because the elementary school that my brother and I would attend was on the other side of our backyard fence. We were five houses down from the alley that went from our neighborhood through to the schoolyard. Usually before school, there were lots of children streaming through that particular walkway to start their day on the playground before the bell signaled that it was time for school to begin. But one spring morning, I was late getting ready for school and had to walk the five-minute journey to school all by myself.

I remember feeling very alone and very tiny as I hurried through the alley and onto the path that led through the playground and into the school itself. I was more than a little bit afraid because I had never been all by myself with such a big expanse of land around me. So I hurried as fast as I could to get to my destination. I got safely through the alley and half way up the path leading to the playground. And then my biggest fear began to unfold before my eyes. I saw the very thing that evoked terror into every part of my little five-year-old body—a giant, fierce-looking dog, and he was running straight toward me! Being the only one in the schoolyard, I was his sole target. I froze in terror as this ferocious animal came bounding across the playground. With his tongue hanging out and his tail wagging, I just knew he was going to bite me mercilessly and devour all my body parts!

As this scruffy dog sniffed my frozen body for what seemed like an eternity, in the distance I heard a voice coming from the direction of the alley I had just passed through. It was little Michael from my kindergarten class. He was also late for school that day and came skipping up the path to see the terror on my face. He said, *"Oh, you don't have to be afraid of this little dog. He won't hurt you!"* As he got to where I stood paralyzed, he leaned over and ran his hand over the dog's head saying, *"See, he's a friendly dog."* And just like a guardian angel, he took my hand, and escorted me away from my traumatic experience, saying, *"Here, I'll walk you to class."*

Michael was a guardian angel, Prince Charming and protector of damsels in distress all wrapped in one package. I was in love! My heart melted with gratitude for his valor and courage that day. I played with him at recess and just knew I had found the one who won my heart—until circle time. That's when little Michael came and sat next to me. As I turned to gaze at his face with stars in my eyes, he decided to spit in my face! The love affair ended forever at that moment in time. My heart was crushed and the prince became a frog once again. I always remained grateful, however, for his help that fateful day, as he saved me from my greatest fear of the furry, ferocious beast on the playground.

I tell this story as a perfect example of a personalized wound. I lived with a very frightening belief instilled in me that dogs were mean and extremely dangerous. Because of that belief, it became my job to keep my distance from them at all costs. Where did I learn such a twisted view of these furry creatures? I learned it as an innocent pre-schooler who played with children slightly older than myself. They decided to tell me something that would scare me, just for the fun of it! In my innocent little mind I reasoned that since they were older, they must have known something I didn't know. So I listened carefully and believed every word of their advice. And when I came face-to-face with one of the ferocious animals they told me about, I responded from my belief that all dogs would devour me, if given the chance. So when I encountered one at a most vulnerable moment in time, my body literally became paralyzed with fear and I was unable to make the forward progress to get to where I needed to be. That is the essence of a personalized wound. It is a belief that twists the truth, creates negative emotions within, and thwarts our forward progress. And who is responsible for these skewed perspectives? As you can probably guess by now, the culprit is once again the enemy of our souls.

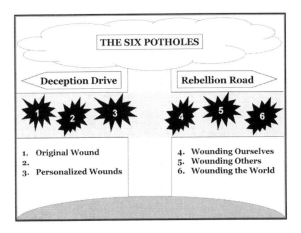

Personalized Wounds are one of the six potholes that trip us up in our walks through life. This particular wound is found on the deception side of the Detour

Road that we have been exploring throughout this series. The first wound we explored was the *Original Wound,* where Satan was able to cause Adam and Eve to give their place of dominion away to him. Then we went all the way to the other side of the Detour Road and examined the pothole called *Wounding the World,* where the full expression of rebellion is manifested in our lives. From there we inspected *Wounding Others* through our judgments. This wound, or pothole, is also on the rebellion side of the Detour Road, and we learned how necessary it is to rid ourselves of this form of sin. In our last book we studied the pothole of *Wounding Ourselves* and identified two ways we receive this wound. First, we wound ourselves through inner vows—the decisions we make that re-write our own laws over God's law written on our hearts. Next, we discovered that we wound ourselves when we do not allow ourselves permission or time to develop the experience of intimacy with God. The lack of heart connection with Him leaves us with a lifeless, legalistic set of rules and regulations we are bound to follow without experiencing His love for us in a tangible way.

The next pothole we encounter is *Personalized Wounds.* Let's find out what these wounds are all about.

Chapter 1

Pothole #3

Introduction to Personalized Wounds

We have finally finished looking at the three potholes of Rebellion Road, where we saw our responsibility for the choices we have made that have wounded others and ourselves. We have crossed over the Highway to Heaven and tasted the goodness of God. Now it is time to find out what the next pothole is that we face on deception's side of the Detour Road.

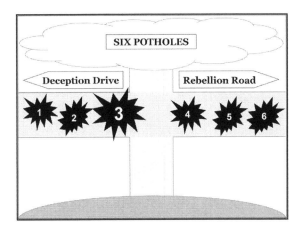

Pothole #3 is entitled Personalized Wounds. As we step off the Highway to Heaven and take our first steps onto Deception Drive, we sense the essence of the wounding change. The focus is no longer on what *we have done to others* (including ourselves), but it is now on what *others have done to us*. This pothole is where wounds are inflicted upon us, and it represents some of the deepest and most damaging wounds to our hearts. Just like inner vows, the wounds are so deep that sometimes we have a difficult time understanding how significantly they impact our everyday lives. That is why it is so important to take time to gain clarity on this deadly pothole.

The primary characteristic of a personalized wound is deception—a personalized wound is designed and intended to deceive us. As they deceive us, they can also paralyze us and keep us from believing the truth, which allows us to step into our intended purposes. Just like my story of encountering the "ferocious" dog, I was paralyzed with fear because of what I believed. My paralysis kept me from my intended destination—my kindergarten classroom. It was only when truth came to the rescue that I was able to continue my forward progress. So it is in our adult lives—when we are deceived, we get pulled off course from the good direction God has for us. [1.1] We falter in living purpose-filled lives because we believe lies instead of truth. And ultimately, the enemy uses these personalized wounds to keep us from our destinies in God.

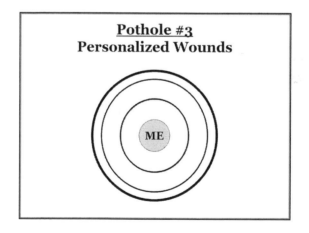

As we see in the picture above, *we* are the target—*the bull's eye*—of personalized wounds. These wounds are unique to our own experience. They are custom fit to our individual lives and circumstances. These personalized wounds affect all four chambers of our hearts, targeting our belief systems, our feelings, the decisions we make and our core identities. They are specifically designed by the enemy to handicap our hearts so we are unable to function from the place of wholeheartedness. This is the strategy of the enemy—to disable our hearts before we are even old enough to understand what has been done. This is the nature of a personalized wound.

I call these personalized wounds, because each of us has our own 100% unique experience of life. There is no one else who has lived life exactly like we have, from our vantage point. Even children raised in the same family, with the same set of circumstances, will have differing views of the same events that occurred in their home. These wounds are, therefore, specific to us, tailor made to fit our individual lives perfectly. The wounds pinpoint our most vulnerable places and sow deception into our hearts to render us incapable of living from a perspective of truth.

Personalized wounds can be compared to the judgments of Pothole #5, which are like the little rocks we find in a garden. We usually have too many personalized wounds to easily count them. Personalized wounds can also be compared to the inner vows of Pothole #4. They are similar in respect to the fact that the subject of the wound is us. Though personalized wounds have similarities to the two other wounds, there is also one significant difference: personalized wounds are *not self-inflicted* wounds. *Others* inflict these wounds upon us. Therefore, we truly are the innocent victims of these wounds, not the perpetrators of them.

Personalized wounds are inflicted upon us in two different realms, usually in close succession and sometimes simultaneously. First we receive personalized wounds in the natural realm, where circumstances cause us emotional or physical pain. Then, either in close succession or even simultaneously, we become wounded in the spiritual realm. When a natural circumstance takes place, almost immediately there is a corresponding event that surrounds and affects us in the invisible, spiritual arena.

Let's return to my dog story as an example. The initial wound that occurred in my own life took place in the natural realm when other children told me that all dogs were vicious. I innocently believed their lie and was wounded emotionally. This in turn opened a door in the spiritual realm for a false belief system to take root in my heart. As that door to my heart opened, the enemy gained access to torment me. In other words, when a personal wound happens to us in the natural realm (either physically or emotionally), the spiritual realm is activated. If we have a strong foundation of truth to combat the spiritual component of the wound, no long lasting injury to our hearts will occur. If we do not have a strong foundation of truth within, however, the enemy is able inflict wounds that last indefinitely and, if severe, cripple our forward progress in that particular area of life.

When these personalized wounds become severe enough, they can lead to *fracturing*. Fracturing is a term used to describe what happens when our hearts suffer extreme trauma or wounding. It is a coping mechanism that causes the heart to break away from the intense physical and emotional pain caused by the wounds, and dissociate from them.

Healing for the fractured heart goes beyond a basic understanding of personalized wounds and, therefore, we must lay a foundation for healing these wounds. In the final chapter of this book, we will take a peak into the realm of "fracturing," but for now let's get back to seeing how these wounds occur, We find an excellent example of the making of a personalized wound in Matthew 13:24-30.

Chapter 2

The Parable of the Wheat and Tares

The Parable

As I was reading my Bible one day, I came upon this parable and suddenly saw it from a completely different perspective. I have never heard anyone teach on the passage from this particular perspective, but it describes our subject very well. So let's read the story Jesus told his followers to discover its application to this wound.

> Vs. 24: *He [Jesus] presented another parable to them, saying, "The kingdom of heaven may be compared to a <u>man</u> who sowed <u>good seed</u> in his <u>field.</u>*

> Vs. 25: *But while <u>men were sleeping,</u> his <u>enemy</u> came and sowed <u>tares</u> also among the wheat, and went away.*

23

Vs. 26: *But when the <u>wheat sprang up and bore grain,</u> then the <u>tares became evident also.</u>*

Vs. 27: *And the slaves of the landowner came and said to him, "Sir, did you now sow good seed in your field? How then does it have tares?"*

Vs. 28: *And he said to them, "An enemy has done this!" And the slaves said to him, "Do you want us, then, to go and gather them up?"*

Vs. 29: *But he said, "No; lest while you are gathering up the tares, you may root up the wheat with them."*

Vs. 30: *Allow both to grow together <u>until the harvest;</u> and in the time of the harvest I will say to <u>the reapers,</u> "First gather up the tares and bind them in bundles to burn them up; but gather <u>the wheat</u> into my barn."*

The Meaning of the Parable

The Parable of the Wheat and Tares
Matthew 13:24-30

The man	=	God
The good seed	=	God's truth
His field	=	Our hearts
Men sleeping	=	Our protectors
The enemy	=	Satan
The tares	=	Satan's lies
As the wheat grew	=	As truth matures
The tares grew up	=	Lies mature also
Evident to the workers	=	Those who know us
Time of harvest	=	When "fruit" ripens
The reapers	=	Those in the body
The wheat	=	God's truth

Let's take a closer look at some of the key words in this parable and find its correlation to personalized wounds.

This is how I understood the parable, verse-by-verse, starting with **verse 24**:

The "man" is God.

The "good seed" is God's truth.

The "field" is our hearts.

So from this verse, we can see that it is God who has sown His truth into our hearts.

Vs. 25:

> The "men sleeping" are the people who were supposed to protect and take care of our hearts, but were not spiritually awakened enough to do so.
>
> The "enemy" is Satan.
>
> The "tares" are Satan's lies.

Our primary caretakers (parents, other significant adults, older siblings, etc.) are the sleeping men. They were given the responsibility to watch over us and protect the seed of God in our hearts, but they were spiritually asleep and were either unaware of their responsibilities or unable to watch everything that happened to us. During the times we were unprotected, the enemy was able to sow lies into our hearts, resulting in a mixture of truth and error growing within each of us.

Vs. 26:

> The "wheat" is God's truth as it matures in us. The fruit of God's truth grows in our hearts and results in our good, pure, godly beliefs.

The "tares" are the lies of the enemy sown next to the good seed of God's truth, which also grow to maturity.

It is important to note that the conflict between the truth and the lies that grows in us becomes "evident" to those around; those who help tend the fields of our hearts.

Vs. 30:

The "time of harvest" is when both the truth and the lies come to maturity in our lives. In other words, when our "fruit ripens," the mixture of truth and error in us becomes noticeable.

The "reapers" are God's workers sent to pull out the lies (or deceptive beliefs) so that God's truth can remain.

The Parable Summary

As we put it all together, this parable is speaking of God's heart for us. He has deposited truth into the fields of our hearts. His words have been written there, just as the prophet Jeremiah told us. [2.1] But as a result of the events in the Garden so long ago, the enemy also has had access to our hearts through spiritual doors that others opened knowingly and unknowingly. Personalized wounds are inflicted upon us when others are "sleeping" or not keeping a close watch to guard us. This leaves the field of our hearts unprotected, which allows the enemy to wound us by depositing seeds of deception into us. These seeds grow into the lies we believe. The lies grow alongside God's good seeds of truth until eventually we can see the mixture of truth and error in ourselves. At that point, we need help tending the fields of our hearts to remove the error that has been able to grow.

Mentors, coaches, counselors, pastors and teachers can come alongside us to bring the tools needed to pull out the weeds of error so truth can prevail. Then, with God's truth pulsing through us, we can be free from the lies that have weighed us down. This is the beauty of receiving healing for our hearts, so that we can move through life free from the wounds that breed the lies. When we rid our hearts of the wounds and the lies, we are able to live wholeheartedly and filled with truth. This was very thing God intended all along.

Chapter 3

The Wounds We Receive =

The Lies We Believe

s we have just seen, personalized wounds become the lies we believe. In order for our hearts to be healed so we can live wholeheartedly, we must find the lies that grow alongside the truth in our hearts and pull them out, so truth can prevail and we can thrive. It's just like weeding a garden—if we do not pull the weeds, they will eventually overtake the yard, choking out the beautiful flowers that have been planted and creating an ugly, overgrown patch of ground, instead of "a little piece of heaven" right in our own backyard. So, let's do some yard work!

What Lies Look Like

Wouldn't it be great if all lies were created equal and if all the "tares" sown into our hearts could be easily seen and removed? That would make life so much simpler. The truth is, however, that some lies are easily seen but unfortunately not all of them are as obvious as others. Satan has had a very long time to perfect his craft of perverting and twisting truth and, therefore, we need to gain an understanding of the different kinds of lies we believe.

I liken lies to eggs—I personally think it's a great analogy! When we go to the grocery store to find eggs, we see that they come in all sizes: small, medium, large and even extra-large. All eggs within each size range have approximately the same amount of calories, grams of protein, fat content, and nutrients. When we purchase the eggs and bring them home to cook, we can make them in a variety of ways. We can scramble, poach, hard or soft boil, and bake them, or we can even use them raw in our favorite recipes. We can even color them if we want to make them look beautiful! But the bottom line is this: an egg, is an egg, is an egg.

Lies are much the same. There are little ones, medium-sized ones, and really big ones. Some are "little white lies" while others are big, dark, ugly ones. We can "cook" lies in many different ways to make them taste good by using them to flavor our circumstances, and we can come out with some great recipes for living. We can even color them when we want to, making them appear to be brilliant and attractive. Lies also have a nutritional affect on our spirits like eggs have on our bodies. Instead of delivering nutrients, however, lies deposit toxins to make our hearts sick and weak instead of healthy and strong. As with eggs, the truth is this: a lie, is a lie, is a lie.

For the sake of giving some clarity to the subject of lies, it would be wise to consider some of the different types of lies we can encounter. This is not by any means an exhaustive list, but it is rather a sampling of the different kinds of lies we can encounter. [3.1]

Lies From Abuse

Some of the most prevalent types of lies we carry in our hearts are beliefs that once were true but now are not. These lies are very often seen in people who were truly victims of abusive behavior in childhood. The abuse could have been verbal, emotional, physical or sexual, but the results are the same. When these individuals were small, they felt powerless to escape their abusive situation. Yet after growing up, victims of abuse still often believe they are powerless to change their circumstances. For instance, a young girl is abused. At the time of the abuse the truth is, *"I can not escape," "I am trapped," "I have no power," "I am helpless."* As she grows up, her circumstances change and she is free from the childhood abuse she experienced. Because of her previous wounding, however, she still believes that she is trapped, helpless and powerless. She makes choices out of those beliefs and ends up in more abusive relationships. As the lies are unveiled and the truth is revealed, she is set free and able to move forward with the power to choose her own destiny.

Lies From Trauma

Another type of lie that is often seen is induced through trauma. We sometimes relate trauma to abuse, but that is not always the case. Trauma is a highly subjective event, and the degree of trauma experienced varies widely from person to person, depending on how each individual is "wired." In one case, a person can experience a major car accident and come out "shaken up," but in the long run he or she may be able to get past the event with only minor emotional upheaval. Another person can experience a "fender bender" and suffer severe emotional repercussions. Whatever wound causes us trauma becomes the catalyst for lies being infused into our hearts, and one traumatic event can infuse many lies into the heart all at once.

Let's say a young boy has a kitten for a pet. The kitten grows up and the young boy and cat have a strong bond between them. Then one day the little boy finds that the cat died while he was away at school. The trauma from the cat's death is the seedbed for many different kinds of lies to be sown, such as, *"Things I love will be taken away," "It's not safe to leave the things I love," "It's my fault my cat died—he wouldn't have died if I had been there," "God must not love me because He let my cat die,"* or *"God killed my cat."* Many lies can be deposited in quick succession when trauma occurs and, therefore, it can take time to gently pull each one out to receive the freedom we are promised.

Lies From Our Environment

We can passively absorb lies that we encounter in our environment. This often occurs when we embrace the wounds of another. Many times, it's a result of long-term exposure to a lifestyle, very similar to the effects of secondhand smoke in our natural environments. With secondhand smoke, we experience a toxic environment, even though we are not the ones polluting it. With environmental lies, we experience a toxic environment as well. The spiritual toxins of others' beliefs and actions pollute our belief systems, and the lies we believe come from what we hear and observe in the environment around us.

Environmental lies can also be one-time events, where we passively absorb a lie from a specific experience that happens. When I was about 8 years old, my recently widowed grandmother decided to take a trip to Hawaii with her girlfriend. Back then, Hawaii had only been a state in the Union for a few years, and there were not multiple flights every day to the islands like there are today. In fact, jets were not used exclusively for commercial flights back then, so Grandma and her girlfriend flew on a four-engine prop plane to and from Hawaii. She spent her vacation exploring the lush beauty of Hawaii and had the time of her life!

When it was time for her to return, our whole family went to the airport to welcome her back home. My parents and my brother and I waited at the airport for her plane to arrive. We waited, and waited, and waited—and then we waited some more. Since air-to-ground radio communications were not as sophisticated as they are today, no one knew why the plane was so late. We ended up waiting for over five hours past her scheduled time of arrival, and I could feel the rising tension in the air as my parents worried silently while they waited. It was not until she finally arrived and began to describe her flight that we understood why she was so late getting back home. They had flown about half way across the Pacific Ocean on their return flight when one of the engines started sputtering and then flared up and quit. They had only three engines left, so it slowed the plane down considerably. Less than an hour after the first engine failed, a second engine started sputtering and finally quit, so now they only had two engines to make it home, which slowed down the plane even more.

Grandma described how she and her girlfriend sat on the plane for hours, wondering if yet another engine or two would stop working. She and her friend silently questioned in their minds if they would make it back, and she described how frightening the experience was for everyone on board. I sat in the back seat of the car and listened to her explain all the details of the flight, and I unknowingly absorbed the fear of her story into my heart. It was not until decades later, when my husband wanted to take me to Hawaii for our tenth wedding anniversary that I felt the effects of the buried fear suddenly surface. I didn't connect the fear, however, with my grandmother's story from decades before—I didn't even remember it! I was puzzled as to why I was suddenly so afraid. I had flown several times before, though never across the ocean. As the day got closer and closer for us to go, a dread rose up within me. It was a terrorizing fear that gripped me from a very deep place inside. I had to force myself to get on the plane, I cried as we took off, and I felt a horrible oppression most of the way there. Then about half an hour before landing, the oppression began to lift and we ended up having one of the best vacations ever!

The same thing happened on our trip home; only then I experienced a very tangible reason to be frightened. Our return flight was taking off, and the airline was showing our departure from Honolulu Airport on a big screen at the front of the plane. We started rolling down the runway, getting up to take-off speed, but instead of lifting off, we continued to roll down the runway long past the time we should have taken off. The water at the end of the runway was getting closer and closer with every second, and the nose of the plane still hadn't lifted upwards. You could feel the growing concern of the passengers on the flight. Finally, at the last second, the pilot slammed on the brakes, reversed the thrust on all three engines and the plane came to a screeching halt dangerously close to the end of the runway.

We found out later that a warning light had come on in the cockpit, causing the pilot to abort the takeoff. We returned to the terminal for repairs, and five hours later a frazzled planeload of people were finally airborne, though the problems were far from resolved. About an hour into the flight, all the lights suddenly went out inside the plane due to an electrical problem. We were flying over the Pacific Ocean in total darkness—so black we couldn't see our hands in front of our faces. Lights came back on but flickered all the way across the Pacific. When our plane finally landed in Seattle, everyone on the plane burst into spontaneous applause, grateful to be on land once again! After that flight, my fear of flying over the ocean was no longer irrational; I had my own terrifying experience about flying across the ocean, which reinforced the fear I absorbed as a child.

We took many more trips across the Pacific Ocean to what became my most beloved destination, and each time we flew the route to Hawaii, I struggled with the same gripping fear. It was not until years later, as I learned about *environmental lies,* that I discovered what had terrorized me for so long. I had been praying for an answer to my dread of flying over water and finally one day, the Lord reminded me of the memory of my grandmother's trip home from Hawaii. I remembered listening to her from the back seat of our car as she relayed the story of her plane ride. I finally got it! I had absorbed the belief that "flying over the ocean is a life-threatening experience." When I saw that my belief came simply by listening to my grandmother's story, I was able to apply the remedy to that belief and my flying experiences across the ocean changed immediately. I was finally able to relax and trust that God would take care of me, just like He had taken care of my grandmother all those years ago.

Lies from Lack [3.2]

So far, the examples of lies have come from bad things that have happened to us, such as abuse, trauma and absorbing the lies of our environment. Those lies are called Type B wounds—"B" represents the *bad things* that happen. But there is another significant type of lie that needs to be addressed before we move on to the remedy. This type of lie comes from *lack*, from an *absence of good* in our formative years. These lies are very different from the others because they are not the result of specific trauma but rather life as it was every day. These are called Type A wounds—"A" represents the absence of the good we should have received. With Type A wounds, there is a lack of nurture and validation. These wounds develop over time, perhaps as a young child who feels ignored by his parents, not being given the emotional or physical nurture needed for healthy self-development. These wounds open the door to the enemy's influence and create the perfect scenario for lies to be sown. When the lack of nurture and validation happens on a daily basis, beliefs such as *"I am not important," "I am not valuable," "I am not wanted,"* and *"I am not loved"* are formed. These beliefs strike at the very core of our spirit chamber, directly attacking our sense of personal identity and causing us to question our worth and purpose for living. When these lies mature, they inhibit our ability to thrive and contribute our unique gifts and talents to the world around us.

Oftentimes someone with Type A wounding cannot identify any specific event or memory that caused the wounds. Instead they feel a sense of numbness. Some have described it as a gray cloud, like a thick fog, that envelops them on the inside. This is an indicator that Type A wounds are present and their resulting lies are buried within. These lies are some of the most difficult to treat because there are no particular events that can be assigned to the lies that are believed. In other words, we cannot pinpoint a place and time when we were wounded and a lie was introduced. Life was just always that way—it was the norm.

Truth vs. Lies

At about this point in time, I can imagine some of you thinking, *"But wait, how can you say what I am believing is a LIE? I was not wanted, I was neglected, I was not valued, no one was there to take care of my emotional or physical needs."* It is time, therefore, for some clarification. When we talk about truth vs. lies, here is the one basic fact we must come into agreement with:

A belief is a lie when it does not line up with God's truth.

To put it differently, God's truth always trumps what our circumstances define as truth. Therefore, even though we experience something that is true (or perceived as true) in the natural realm, there is a higher truth that prevails in the spiritual realm. The higher truth comes from God's kingdom and it is eternal truth.

An Example

For example, let's say little Johnny was truly neglected by his parents and was emotionally and physically abandoned. He lives with the reality that Dad abandoned him at age two because he didn't want the responsibility of a "kid," and Mom gave him to relatives to raise, so she could "start over." Johnny was truly unwanted and unloved by his natural parents. He grew up with huge deficits of nurture, love, and self-worth.

Little Renee's situation, however, was completely different. Her parents did love her, but for a variety of reasons they could not give her the time or attention she needed. Dad was in the military, and he was given multiple assignments overseas when Renee turned 2 years old. As a result, he was gone for a good portion of her formative years. Mom tried to make up for the lack of Dad's influence in the home, but she had a fulltime job and three other children to care for. She worked 10 hours a day, five days a week just to help make ends meet. There were simply not enough hours in the day to give little Renee all the nurture, love and attention she needed. As Renee grew, a deep sense of being unwanted, unloved, and invaluable took hold in her heart.

These two children had completely different scenarios, yet in both cases, they were both wounded by emotional and physical abandonment. The resulting lie sown into their hearts was the same: *"I am not loved, wanted or valuable."*

It is a lie because in both cases there is a *higher truth* that prevails. *God's truth* is that He has an extravagant love for Johnny and Renee. God wanted them to understand His love for them from their earliest days on earth. For a multitude of reasons, they did not get the message. Instead, they were deprived of the higher truth and concluded their own "truth" from their circumstances. Johnny lived in the natural truth that he was unloved because of his abandonment. Renee believed the bold-faced lie that she was unloved. Both children perceived these lies as truth because of their experiences, yet both needed the revelation of God's higher truth to replace the lies that had damaged their hearts for so long. When that revelation comes, their hearts can receive the healing they need.

Summary

As we look at the lies that come from lack, it is important to restate that in the natural realm, these beliefs might be true, but in the spiritual realm, these beliefs are the lies.

As we endeavor to find God's eternal truth that supersedes the natural truth, our hearts are positioned to receive healing.

Having established an understanding of truth vs. lies, there is one more thing we must know. The circumstantial truth, or natural truth, of Johnny and Renee's lives must be validated. The pain of their circumstances, and resulting wounds to their hearts, should never be minimized or discounted in the least. Whether our wound is valid, or is just our own perception of the truth, the negative emotions we feel need three things, which I learned as we studied the emotional chamber of the heart in Book #1. Negative emotions must be:

1. Expressed

2. Validated

3. Resolved

We are going to find out how to accomplish those three things in the next chapter.

Evaluating Your Heart

Before we move ahead to finding the specific lies we have believed, it would be a good idea to spend a few minutes personally evaluating your own heart based on the information of this chapter. Taking the time to thoughtfully write down the answers to the questions below will help you look toward healing for the lies you have personally believed.

Were you able to identify any beliefs that would be considered lies from God's perspective? If so, which categories did they fall into?

- Lies from abuse?

- Lies from trauma?

- Lies from environment?

- Lies from lack?

There are many more types of lies that could be studied, [3.1] but the point we need to embrace is this: The lies we believe come from the kinds of wounds we receive. With that understanding in place, let's take a look at the clues that lead us to the lies we believe.

Chapter 4

The Clues that Lead Us to the Lies

Sometimes it is easy to see the wounds we have received and the resulting lies that we have come to believe, like those we identified in the last chapter. But with the variety of lies that can be planted inside our hearts, it can sometimes feel overwhelming to think of trying to find all the different lies planted and then rid our "fields" of all those "weeds." There should be an easy way to find these weeds and pull them out—and fortunately there is. The good news is that God has already given us the clues we need to find the lies we believe. And these clues are found right under our noses—right within our own hearts. *"So what are these clues?"* you may ask. The clues are our emotions.

Emotions: The Gauges of our Hearts

If you remember all the way back to our first book, we discovered how each of the four chambers of the heart functions. In the emotional chamber, we learned that emotions were gauges as to what goes on inside our hearts. They let us know when something needs attention just like the indicators on a car's dashboard. Our positive emotions indicate we are doing well and are living from the happy place of a healthy heart. Negative emotions indicate we have a problem with something inside that needs to be fixed. The "something" can be a lie, though that is not always the case. When it is a lie, we need to apply "the fix" to bring us back to a place of operating as we are intended. Yet before we look at the emotions that lead us to the lies we believe, let's look at the four categories of emotions in general.

The Four Categories of Emotions

Categorizing emotions is a lifesaver for people who live with an acute awareness of their emotions. These people are known in different circles as "feelers," "burden bearers," "intercessors," "perceivers," "intuitives," and probably other names. Most often, women are attributed with the stereotype of being the emotional ones, but what I have found to be true in my counseling career is that many men are every bit as emotional as women. Unfortunately, there is a lesser tolerance for emotional men in our culture, and therefore we find men who have never been taught how to manage their emotions, resulting in the denial of the emotional part of their hearts. For these kinds of people (male or female), emotions can be overwhelming, leading to a complete shutdown of emotions at one end of a spectrum or to emotional overload and breakdowns at the other end. The chart below will help make sense of the gift of emotions God has given to each of us. It shows us how we can categorize our emotions and what to do with the bothersome ones we experience. Sorting out our emotions enables us to live with internal order and peace instead of chaos. And what we will discover shortly is that one set of these emotions actually leads us to the lies we believe.

Four Categories of Emotions

GOD'S INTENDED EMOTIONS

Acceptance *Strength*
Joy/Peace *Hope/Purpose*
Honor *Purity* *Value* *Clarity*

SATAN'S OPPOSING EMOTIONS	TRUTH-BASED EMOTIONS	VENGEFUL EMOTIONS
1. Fear	1. Sadness	1. Resentment
2. Rejection	2. Loneliness	2. Bitterness
3. Shame	3. Sorrow	3. Judgmental Attitudes
4. Guilt	4. Disgust	4. *Unrighteous Anger
5. Weakness	5. Disappointment	5. Condemnation
6. Worthlessness	6. Conviction	6. Rebellion
7. Confusion	7. Loss	7. *Depression
8. Hopelessness	8. Righteous Anger	8. Hatred
	9. Emotional Numbness	

1) God's Intended Emotions

From the chart, we see our picture again, with the cloud at the top representing heaven. Inside the cloud are God's Intended Emotions for us. These are the emotions of joy & peace, acceptance, honor, purity, strength, value, clarity, hope and purpose. These emotions are the goal we all want to achieve and sustain. They are the life-sustaining emotions God intended us to feel from the very beginning of time. They are just like the joyous emotions that were stirred up on the Highway to Heaven, as we focused our attention on what awaits us in eternity. They are a taste of heaven and the very emotions God wants us to experience here on earth. This is the target we shoot for, and when we hit the target, we deeply feel the sense of being fully alive and whole within our hearts.

2) Truth-Based Emotions

On the chart, directly below the cloud, at the intersection of the Highway to Heaven and the Detour Road, we see Truth-Based Emotions. These emotions are the result of the effects of the fall in the Garden of Eden. They are based in truth but represent the consequences of the fall brought on mankind, such as loss, grief, and unfulfilled dreams and desires. These emotions include, sadness, loneliness, sorrow, disgust, disappointment, conviction (feeling guilty for sin which we have done), loss, righteous anger, and even emotional numbness, which is associated with shock and trauma. These emotions are the ones we experience based in the natural truth of our circumstances. For example, we grieve when a loved one dies. We were not personally responsible for the death of our loved one, but the grief comes from the reality of death, which is a consequence of the fallen nature of mankind.

Another example is loneliness. Let's say Tim's wife Lisa left him. She got tired of the confinement and responsibility of marriage, so she packed up her things while Tim was away at work and moved out without leaving so much as a note to let him know she was leaving him. Tim came home to find all of her belongings gone—he was left devastated. He was a great husband, dedicated and sacrificial, but Lisa wanted a different lifestyle. Tim felt a flood of emotions, but over time the net result was deep loneliness because he lost the companionship that God planned for him from the beginning of time. He didn't do anything to warrant this loneliness, but the present truth is that he is not experiencing what God intended for him due to the choices his wife made. The loneliness he feels is based in the natural truth that his wife left him and he is now alone. His heart needs a specific type of healing from this truth-based emotion.

To find healing for truth-based emotions, the first thing we must do is to simply own the emotions, express them to the Lord and invite Him to bring the restoration necessary to heal our hearts. As I counsel others, I encourage my clients to identify the specific emotions they feel in this category: grief, sadness, loneliness, and so on. Once we have pinpointed the specific emotion or emotions, I ask them to give those emotions to God as they pray. Sometimes clients symbolically cup their hands together, holding their pain, and then extend their hands, prayerfully surrendering to the Lord the emotions they have held for so long.

Then we pray together and ask God what He wants to give the person in return for the pain that was just given to Him. Because Jesus has told us that His sheep hear His voice and will not follow the voice of another, [4.1] we can proceed with the confidence that He will speak to their hearts. Our confidence comes also from the truth Jesus told his followers:

> *"Ask, and it shall be given to you...what man is*
> *there among you, when his son shall ask him for*
> *a loaf, will give him a stone? Or if he shall ask*
> *for a fish, he will not give him a snake, will he?*
> *If you then, being evil, know how to give good*
> *gifts to your children, how much more shall*
> *your Father who is in heaven give what is good*
> *to those who ask Him!* [4.2]

With an assurance that He speaks to our hearts, [4.3] we wait to hear His answer. Once we hear an answer, we always "test the spirits", [4.4] making certain what we hear aligns with God's truth. If it does, it passes the test, and they can receive the truth into their hearts and ask Jesus to heal the broken place.

I have found that each time a client hears a response from the Lord, it is different. The response is unique to each person's particular situation. But regardless of what the response is, they come away with tremendous comfort, peace, and even joy in their hearts. And if a client doesn't sense a response from the Lord, we step into a place of faith, [(4.5)] believing He is accomplishing the necessary work of healing the heart.

One time I asked a client to pray, giving the grief of a loved one's death to the Lord. As we asked what God wanted to give her in return for her pain, she heard the Lord speak to her heart in response to our question. Suddenly she was completely set free from all of her grief, all sense of loss, and all the pain surrounding the death. It happened in an instant! I checked back with her a couple of weeks later and the pain was still gone— it never returned! God had instantly healed her heart and brought her to a place of being able to move forward with her life after the tragic death of her loved one. That is just one powerful example of the healing I have witnessed as I have used this chart to help people identify and appropriately resolve the negative emotions they feel.

3) Vengeful Emotions

Next, on the right hand side of the chart (Rebellion Road) we see Vengeful Emotions. These are the emotions we experience when we have fallen into one of the potholes on rebellion's side of the Detour Road.

These emotions include resentment, bitterness, judgmental attitudes, unrighteous anger, condemnation, rebellion, depression and hatred. Since we have already learned how to resolve rebellion from Book #3, let's review and apply the tool to rebellious emotions.

To bring healing to the rebellious emotions we feel, we use the tools of the 5 R's—Repent, Release, Renounce—and apply the appropriate prayer to the emotions we are experiencing. For instance, *"God, I repent for my <u>bitterness</u> toward* Jessica. *I release her from <u>any debt I feel she owes me</u> and forgive her for the ways she has wronged me. I renounce my partnership with any demonic spirits empowering the bitterness toward her and command them to leave me now. Instead I choose bless her.* [(4.6)] *I ask you to restore love, joy and peace in my heart once again."* Going through that exercise will diminish the vengeful emotions that are present. Different emotions may arise from other categories once those are dealt with, and if they do, applying the appropriate remedies we are learning to the other categories will restore our hearts back to God's intended emotions for us.

4) Satan's Opposing Emotions

On the left side of the chart is Deception Drive, and we see Satan's Opposing Emotions. These are the emotions we focus on in order to find the lies lodged in our hearts. They are on the deception side of the Detour Road, because they represent the emotions we feel when we are being deceived into believing Satan's lies instead of God's truth. If we remember way back to Book #2, when the Fall occurred in the Garden, these are the emotions Satan brought to bear on Adam and Eve, to replace God's intended emotions for them with his own set of emotions. They include fear, rejection, shame, guilt, weakness, worthlessness, confusion, and hopelessness. These specific emotions are the clues that lead us to the lies we believe. Using these specific emotions as a guide, in the next chapter we will begin the work of finding the lies lodged within our hearts.

Chart Summary

When we use this chart of the four categories of emotions, we quickly discover what is happening in our hearts from an emotional perspective. Usually emotions are some of the first things we identify and connect with in our hearts, so this tool gives us a streamlined way to organize our emotions and measure what is happening on the inside. When we match our emotions to the appropriate category, we can easily begin a dialog with God as to how to bring our hearts to a place of peace and joy with Him. This may sound too objective and scientific for some, but for those who are either extremely emotional or extremely analytical in nature, this is an effective and efficient way to balance out our emotions and bring us the peace our hearts are desperately longing to have.

Two Exceptions: Anger and Depression

There is always an exception to every rule, and the subject of emotions is no different. Most of us experience two particular emotions that can cause confusion when we are evaluating them from the emotional chart listed above. This is because they are "tricky" emotions, ones that can mask the real issues going on in our hearts. They are tricky because they are considered secondary emotions, ones that arise as a result of other primary emotions being present. First, let's take a look at the emotion of anger.

Anger

Anger is a tricky emotion to process for this reason: we can have two kinds of anger—righteous or unrighteous. Righteous anger expresses appropriate displeasure for that which is unjust, immoral, and unholy. It is a moral indignation, which is what Jesus displayed when He went into the temple and overturned the tables where people were selling goods to profit themselves. (4.7) He was righteously indignant because the purpose of the temple as a house of worship and prayer had been reduced to a place of personal profit. Since Jesus was both God and a man who lived a sinless life on earth, we know that He was not sinning when He expressed His righteous indignation or anger. From His example, we can also know that in today's world we are not sinning when we express righteous anger or indignation.

Unrighteous anger, however, is an emotion the enemy offers us as a tool. If we partner with this tool, we use inappropriate expressions of anger for the purpose of intimidation and revenge. This type of anger is abusive and vengeful in nature. It is a selfish kind of anger that seeks to express hateful thoughts and emotions as retribution or "payback." It rises up as a reaction to wounding. When someone hurts us, we protect our hearts and cover the pain by lashing out in unrighteous anger toward the offender instead of identifying the wound and seeking healing. That is the reason this type of anger is called a secondary emotion, because the primary emotion is pain that stems from the initial wound we receive. We ignore the initial pain and express it as anger. This type of anger is sin and we need to repent of it.

Both types of anger can also be reactions to injustice, whether it is an injustice inflicted upon us or upon others. We briefly looked at the progression of how anger turns from a righteous response to an unrighteous one in Book #4 when we studied Judgments. In Chapter One, we read:

> *"This sense of justice is a seed from the Garden that still resides within us. From that seed, we identify with the heart of God—"the Ideal" we learned about in Book #2. We still carry our heavenly Father's DNA and we long for justice and goodness to prevail. So when we experience the opposite of what we long for, our sense of justice is violated. We immediately feel injustice pierce our hearts and we are grieved. We want the wrong, righted. So in reality our hearts start out in the right place. But ever so quickly, we take justice into our own hands, as we judge the guilty party. Even though our hearts start out in the right place—when we carry out our own justice by judging—we do so in an unjust manner."* (4.8)

Judging is just one way that unrighteous anger is expressed. It is also expressed as the Vengeful Emotions on the chart we just studied. If you look closely at the list, there was one other emotion that seemed out of place. It is our next "tricky" emotion.

Depression

Depression is as widespread as the common cold. It is a condition that can strike at any time—it can come and go like the wind or it can park over us like a foreboding oppression. Sometimes the reasons for its presence can be difficult to identify. For some people, it is physiological in nature. There are conditions, such as imbalances of certain chemicals in the brain that can cause symptoms of depression. There are also environmental conditions that affect many people. I lived in Washington State for 25 years, and I experienced first-hand the physical effects of a lack of sunshine for 10 months out of the year. I came to know my particular depression as SAD—Seasonal Affective Disorder. It brought a sense of lethargy, low-grade depression, lack of motivation and a continual desire to sleep whenever the dreary weather would come (which was a great majority of time). The minute the sun started shining, my depression would lift and I felt like I had been infused with a super vitamin as I suddenly came to life again. I lived my life for many years just longing for the sun to shine, so I could feel like I was alive inside.

But there are also spiritual reasons for depression. Those spiritual reasons are rooted either in deception or in rebellion, depending on the underlying emotions. So let's look first at depression rooted in deception.

Depression as Deception

When we look at our emotional chart, under Satan's Opposing Emotions (on the Deception side of the Detour Road), we see eight different emotions listed. They are: fear, rejection, shame, guilt, weakness, worthlessness, confusion, and hopelessness. As we have already learned, these emotions are attached to the lies we believe. What is also vital to note is that depression is *not* on that list. Why? Depression is the *result* of these negative emotions. It is like a covering, placed over something that has already been set in place. Depression can be compared to layering our clothes when we dress for the day. Those who come from climates where temperatures change rapidly are very aware of the need to dress in layers: a tank top is the first layer, a long-sleeved shirt over the tank top, then maybe a comfortable vest over the shirt, and finally a coat over the vest. All those layers are needed to accommodate for the weather changes in a day. Depression is a layer that covers the emotional layers underneath it. To say it another way: *depression* is *oppression*. It covers the primary emotions listed on Deception Drive and, therefore, it is a secondary emotion.

To site an example of this in the Bible, the prophet Isaiah told us, *"In righteousness you will be established; you will be far from oppression, for you will not fear."* (4.9) When we look closely at that verse, we see that oppression is the result of fear. God is telling us through the words of Isaiah that when we get rid of fear, oppression will not be able to get close to us. In other words, fear opens the door to oppression. Fear and oppression are two separate things and one follows the other. When we deal with the underlying cause (the fear, shame, guilt, etc.), the access doors are closed and the enemy has no way to get into our hearts to oppress us with depression.

Depression as Rebellion

Depression can also be rooted in rebellion. There is an intriguing twist to this particular expression of depression, and it is best described by looking at the ancient account of Cain and Abel.

After Adam and Eve were driven out of the Garden of Eden, they had two sons. The first they named Cain and the second they named Abel. Abel was a shepherd (*"keeper of sheep"*) and Cain was a farmer (*"tiller of the ground"*). One day, Cain brought an offering to the Lord from the fruit of the ground, likely the produce he had grown with his own hands. And Abel brought an offering to the Lord from the flocks he tended.

The text says, *"…the LORD had respect and regard for Abel and for his offering. But for Cain and his offering, He had no respect or regard. (4.10) So Cain was exceedingly angry and indignant, and he looked sad and depressed. And the LORD said to Cain, 'Why are you angry? And why do you look sad and depressed and dejected? If you do well, will you not be accepted? And if you do not do well, sin crouches at your door; its desire is for you, but you must master it.'"* (4.11)

Let's stop here to highlight the interchange God had with Cain. When Cain's offering was rejected, the Lord Himself spoke to him. First He asked two questions, followed by some very direct instruction. God asked, *"Why are you angry?"* and then, *"Why do you look sad and depressed and dejected?"* God was pointing out that his countenance didn't match what was happening in his heart. He looked sad and depressed but God pointed out the real issue was his anger. When God gave Cain a solution to his problem, by telling him he could redeem his situation, Cain ignored God's advice and chose to go his own way. He *rebelled* against the grace of God, held onto his anger and killed his brother instead.

This is a perfect example of depression rooted in rebellion. Depression is sometimes a cover-up for an unrepentant heart. It can be an indicator that we have unforgiveness lodged in our hearts and an unwillingness to let go of an offense done to us. Where there is an unwillingness to forgive, we can be sure that there is an even deeper root of pride, and perhaps even self-protection that exists, that must be extricated in order for us to find relief from the depths of the demonic strongholds of depression. Therefore, when we are struggling with depression, in order to find the healing God wants to bring to us, we must be willing to ask the Lord what our depression is rooted in. Is it rooted in a lie we believe? Or is it rooted in unrighteous anger and rebellion? Are there components of pride, unforgiveness, or self-protection attached to our depression? As the Holy Spirit reveals the answers to our questions, we can apply the appropriate remedies, and the stronghold of depression will be demolished in our hearts.

Summary

Emotions are the clues that lead us to find what really resides within our hearts. There are four categories of emotions. God's Intended Emotions is the first category, and they are the joyful ones that express the emotions He intended us to experience on a continual basis. Then there are Truth-Based Emotions— those we experience in our natural circumstances, which are the result of the fallen nature we all carry. Next is the category of Vengeful Emotions. These are the feelings we experience when we partner with the enemy and take on his tools for dealing with wounds that others inflict upon us. They are rebellious in nature, causing us to retaliate in order to payback "evil for evil." The fourth category is Satan's Opposing Emotions—those that oppose the truth of God and indicate that deception has taken root in our hearts. Finally, we can experience the tricky nature of both anger and depression. Anger can be righteous or unrighteous in nature, and if it is unrighteous or sinful, we must eradicate it through our repentance. Depression has a differing dynamic to it and is either rooted in deception or rebellion. It takes our partnership with the Holy Spirit to discover the roots of our depression and then apply the remedies to it for our freedom to be manifested in our lives.

Evaluating Your Heart

This chapter has taken the lid off of a very deep well—the well of our emotions. Perhaps all kinds of feelings have been uncovered that may have been buried for years. So before we go farther, let's take some time to process what we have uncovered this far. Answer the questions as honestly as you can before moving forward to the next chapter.

1. From the category of God's Intended Emotions, what are the good, healthy emotions that you feel on a regular basis?

2. When do those emotions most often occur?

3. What activities bring those emotions to the surface most effectively?

4. With which of the truth-based emotions do you identify?

5. Are there certain times of the day or certain events that bring these emotions to the surface?

6. Have you taken time in the past to pray through these emotions?

7. Have you offered them to the Lord, asking Him what He would like to give you in exchange for them?

8. Of the vengeful emotions listed, which of them most often bother you?

9. When do they surface?

10. Do you understand what events take place that trigger those vengeful emotions?

11. Have you taken the time to repent for partnering with the enemy's emotions?

12. Which of the two "tricky" emotions do you identify with?

13. Do you find yourself frequently angry?

14. If so, what is the cause of your anger?

15. How do you manage your anger?

16. What are the steps you have taken to minimize your anger?

17. Have you repented for the anger you continue to carry in your heart?

18. Do you find yourself frequently depressed?

19. If so, where do you feel the depression is rooted—on the deception side or the rebellion side of the detour?

20. If depression is masking anger or unforgiveness in your heart, have you taken that to the Lord and repented?

21. Have you forgiven those who have hurt you?

Once you answer the questions as honestly as you can and pray through the remedies previously mentioned to the best of your ability, you will be ready to uncover the lies that have been sown into your heart. We begin that process in the next chapter.

Chapter 5

Healing Personalized Wounds

In this chapter we are going to continue going into the very deepest places of the heart, where the rewards are great for this part of our journey. We are finally going to find the lies the enemy has sown into our hearts as we do one final evaluation.

It's time to find out how our hearts receive the healing from the personal wounds we have all received. To do so, we will begin by looking at the chart that was originally introduced in Book #2. If you remember, the chart showed us the original atmosphere that Adam and Eve lived in the Garden of Eden, as well as the atmosphere that was produced once they disobeyed God.

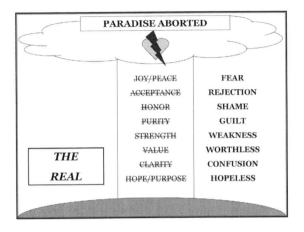

	JOY/PEACE	FEAR
	ACCEPTANCE	REJECTION
	HONOR	SHAME
	PURITY	GUILT
	STRENGTH	WEAKNESS
THE	VALUE	WORTHLESS
	CLARITY	CONFUSION
REAL	HOPE/PURPOSE	HOPELESS

In order to discover where the lies are lodged within our hearts, we will be looking at the eight categories of contrasting emotions represented in this chart. For instance, the first category is the contrasting emotions of Joy/Peace and Fear. The column on the left represents God's Intended Emotions for us and the column on the right represents Satan's Opposing Emotions. The next section contains a self-evaluation chart for each of the eight categories. You will have to keep track of your answers on a separate sheet of paper if you have an ebook copy of this book. Follow the directions below and complete all eight categories of emotions before reading the section eentitled "Steps for Healing", as it will give you the benefit of unbiased answers.

Directions for Taking the Self-Evaluation

To take this self-evaluation, simply start with the first group of emotions, Joy & Peace vs. Fear. Compare the positive emotion with the negative one on each line by asking yourself: *"Do I generally feel _____ or _____?"* For example, the first line is:

Assured or Intimidated

1. Ask yourself, *"Do I generally feel **assured** or **intimidated**?"* Make note of the box that best fits your answer.

2. If you feel *Assured* **all** of the time, make note of the "**A**" box closest to *Assured*. If you feel *Intimidated* **all** of the time, make note of the "**A**" box next to *Intimidated*.

3. If you feel one of the emotions **most** of the time, make note of the "**M**" box closest to the word that describes you best.

4. If you do not feel either emotion strongly, make note of the "**N**" in the middle for **Neutral**.

Once you complete each of the eight categories, identify the categories that have the most negative responses to the emotions presented. For example, in the category of **Honor vs. Shame,** if you had 7 answers that favored **Shame** and 3 answers that favored **Honor,** this would be a category that you would want to highlight for further work. Identifying the categories with the most negative responses is going to help you discover the lies that are lodged within.

Emotional Chart #1

PEACE vs. FEAR

	A	M	N	M	A	
Assured						Intimidated
Calm						Nervous
Contented						Tormented
Courageous						Cowardly
Fearless						Afraid
Peaceful						Panicked
Serene						Agitated
Tranquil						Anxious
Understood						Misunderstood
Unguarded						Suspicious

Mark the degree of your dominant emotion as you answer this question:
"In a general sense, do I primarily feel ___ or ___?"

A = Always   M = Most of the Time   N = Neutral

Emotional Chart #2

ACCEPTED vs. REJECTED

	A	M	N	M	A	
Belonging						Alone
Embraced						Rejected
Found						Abandoned
Given a place						Displaced
Included						Left out
Kept						Discarded
Preserved						Ruined
Accepted						Pushed aside
Remembered						Forgotten
Seen						Invisible

Mark the degree of your dominant emotion as you answer this question:
"In a general sense, do I primarily feel ___ or ___?"

A = Always   M = Most of the Time   N = Neutral

Copyright 2008 by Heart of Healing Ministries
All Rights Reserved. Do not reproduce without written permission.

Emotional Chart #3

HONOR vs. SHAME

	A	M	N	M	A	
Applauded						Shamed
Approved						Rejected
Delightful						Irritating
Elevated						Humiliated
Esteemed						Disdained
Honored						Disgraced
Pleasing						Annoying
Respected						Belittled
Whole						Damaged
Wise						Foolish

Mark the degree of your dominant emotion as you answer this question:
"In a general sense, do I primarily feel ___ or ___?"

A = Always   M = Most of the Time   N = Neutral

Copyright 2008 by Heart of Healing Ministries
All Rights Reserved. Do not reproduce without written permission.

Emotional Chart #4

PURITY vs. GUILT

	A	M	N	M	A	
Blessed						Cursed
Celebrated						Scorned
Clean						Dirty
Flawless						Inferior
Innocent						Guilty
Perfect						Flawed
Pure						Tainted
Shiny						Tarnished
Sinless						Damned
Wholesome						Corrupted

Mark the degree of your dominant emotion as you answer this question:
"In a general sense, do I primarily feel ___ or ___?"

A = Always   M = Most of the Time   N = Neutral

Emotional Chart #5

STRENGTH vs. WEAKNESS

	A	M	N	M	A	
Empowered						Exhausted
Free						Trapped
Grown up						Little
Mighty						Powerless
Powerful						Helpless
Protected						Vulnerable
Safe						Endangered
Sheltered						Defenseless
Shielded						Uncovered
Strong						Weak

Mark the degree of your dominant emotion as you answer this question:
"In a general sense, do I primarily feel ___ or ___?"

A = Always   M = Most of the Time   N = Neutral

Emotional Chart #6

VALUE vs. WORTHLESS

	A	M	N	M	A	
Adored						Unloved
Cared for						Mistreated
Liked						Disliked
Recognized						Ignored
Suitable						Unfit
Supported						Opposed
Treasured						Devalued
Trusted						Doubted
Valued						Worthless
Worthy						Undeserving

Mark the degree of your dominant emotion as you answer this question:
"In a general sense, do I primarily feel ____ or ____?"

A = Always   M = Most of the Time   N = Neutral

Emotional Chart #7

CLARITY vs. CONFUSION

	A	M	N	M	A	
Certain						Doubtful
Thinking clearly						Uncertain
Comprehending						Confounded
Decisive						Ambivalent
Definite						Indecisive
Discerning						Confused
Enlightened						Bewildered
Sane						Crazy
Sure						Undecided
Understanding						Perplexed

Mark the degree of your dominant emotion as you answer this question:
"In a general sense, do I primarily feel ____ or ____?"

A = Always   M = Most of the Time   N = Neutral

Emotional Chart #8

PURPOSE vs. HOPELESS

	A	M	N	M	A	
Cheerful						Sad
Energized						Fatigued
Enthused						Apathetic
Invigorated						Weary
Optimistic						Hopeless
Passionate						Indifferent
Sensitive						Insensitive
Successful						Failure
Triumphant						Defeated
Victorious						Beaten

Mark the degree of your dominant emotion as you answer this question:
"In a general sense, do I primarily feel ____ or ____?"

A = Always   M = Most of the Time   N = Neutral

In the next section, we will be identifying some of the "weeds" in our fields, or some of the lies, that continue to be lodged within our hearts. We will also learn how to pull these "weeds" and have the "good seed" sown in its place.

Steps for Healing

Step One:

As you look at your evaluation, find the group or groups that have the most marks closest to the negative side—Satan's Opposing Emotions. If there are several groups, begin with the one that has the most negative responses.

Step Two:

On a piece of paper, title a blank sheet: "Lies I Believe." Then, find a quiet place and have the following dialog with the Lord:

> *"Lord, will You come by way of Your Holy Spirit and direct me?"*

Wait for a sense of His presence. When You can sense His presence, continue with the dialog. If, after a few minutes, you do not feel a sense of His presence, proceed with the dialog in faith, believing He is listening to you.

> *"I feel _____ (name the category you chose, such as fear, shame, hopelessness, etc.) What is the lie I'm believing?"*

Again, this is a time to listen. A thought might come to mind, or a memory of a childhood experience, or another impression might surface. Do not dismiss these thoughts, but rather listen for the Lord and focus carefully on your dialog with Him. When a belief you hold that is contrary to God's truth comes to mind, write it down on the "Lies I Believe" chart. You can repeat the process as many times as you want to in order to find multiple lies. Or you can pray through each individual lie before moving on to the next using the following prayer.

Step Three:

Pray the following prayer to pull out the lies of the enemy from the field of your heart.

Prayer for Lies:

"Lord, I repent for coming into agreement with the lie that _____.

I release (forgive) _____ who opened the door for the lie to be sown into my heart.

I renounce the lie that _____ (example: "I am alone.")

I break all agreement with the enemy who has empowered the lie and command all demonic forces to leave me now, in Jesus' name.

Lord, what is YOUR truth that replaces this lie?"

WAIT and LISTEN. Do not assume you know what the Lord will say to you, and do not rush to quote an appropriate scripture. Just listen and wait *until He* speaks.

When you hear the truth, it will bring peace, comfort and joy to your heart. As you feel the truth in your spirit, respond to it.

> *"Lord, I receive Your truth into my heart to replace the lie I have believed. Thank You for giving me the truth and healing the wounded place of my heart."*

Summary of Healing the Lies

This exercise should be done over time for all eight groups of emotions. It is not intended to be done all at once because, as we have already learned, these wounds are much like judgments—there are probably many of them to find. As the Lord leads you to return to this exercise, you can know you have the tools to effectively be the gardener of your own heart.

For some who are new to listening to the Holy Spirit with their own spirit, this exercise might be challenging, but I encourage you to try. You might be thoroughly amazed at the insight you receive from Him. After all, God's Word says that God sent the Holy Spirit to lead and guide us into *all* truth. You will want to make sure what you hear lines up with the truth of God's written word to make sure you stay on the right path. If you are unsure, you can always find a friend whom you trust and do this exercise together.

Each time you do this exercise write down what happened as a result. Perhaps you had a definitive response from the Lord. Or maybe you had some thoughts come to mind but you are not sure whether it was the Holy Spirit speaking to you or your own mind. If so, continue to pray into those thoughts and steward them prayerfully before the Lord. In time, you will hear more clearly and become more confident in this simple process to true freedom. As an added step, I encourage you to send in your stories of breakthrough via our web site contact page.

The "5 R's"

Since we have found some of the "weeds" that were sown into our hearts from long ago, it is time to put yet another tool into our tool belts, so that we are adequately prepared for whatever we may find in the future.

In the previous books, we have used the 5 R's chart to find the remedies for wounding the world through rebellion, wounding others through judgments and wounding ourselves through inner vows. Those remedies include combinations of repentance, releasing others through forgiveness and renouncing our partnership with the demonic realm. Now it's time to identify the fourth of our 5 R's—Receive.

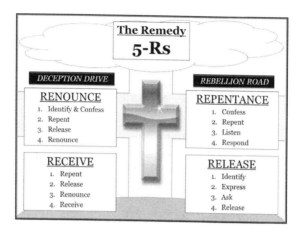

Looking at the *Prayer for Lies* in the previous section, we see that in order to rid our hearts of the lies we have believed, we first use the three "R's" we have already learned—Repent, Release, Renounce. Then we add the fourth "R"—Receive. After we renounce our agreement with the enemy who empowers the lies in our hearts, we ask the Lord for the truth that will replace the lie. When we hear the truth from Him, we actively receive it, by asking God to plant that good seed of truth into our hearts. Once we have asked God to plant the truth in place of the lies, we take a step of faith and thank Him for doing so. Many times people will feel a shift in their hearts by way of their emotions or thoughts. Even if nothing feels differently, our step of faith to receive the truth pleases Him. (5.1) Acknowledging God's activity in our hearts allows us to step into the belief that He is accomplishing the work of healing the wounds of our hearts. That is what He said He would do.

As the chart indicates, the 4 steps for our fourth "R" — *Receive* — are as follows:

1. *Repent* for coming into agreement with the lie(s).

2. *Release* (by forgiving) those who were responsible for allowing the enemy to sow lies into your heart.

3. *Renounce* all partnership with the demonic realm.

4. *Receive* the truth. Ask God for the truth to replace the lies and welcome it into your heart.

Summary

This chapter has been all about following the clues of our emotions to the places where the lies were implanted into our hearts. As we looked at the eight categories of emotions, we were able to identify the categories that represented the most lies found within. Then we dialoged with the Lord and asked Him to lead us to the source of the lies. Once He spoke, we used the Prayer for Lies to eradicate them from our hearts. Finally we put the fourth "R" in place in the 5 R's chart. We only have one left to learn, and that will happen in the next book of the series.

With those truths set in place, we are now ready to take a step forward into a deeper layer of our hearts as we explore the arena of the deeply broken or fractured heart. This is a place where many precious people spend a significant portion of their lives.

Chapter Six

The Fractured Heart

I am including this chapter for those who want some clarification on the somber effects of the deeply wounded heart. Though I am not an expert on this subject, I have worked with many people who have had their hearts severely broken, or "fractured." Therefore, I wanted to include a brief explanation of this subject from my perspective. I include it in this particular book because fractures are the result of personalized wounds. These wounds, however, are usually much more harsh than others and violate a person at the deepest places of the heart.

Most often, those who have experienced a fracturing of the heart need the help of a counselor or other trained professionals to fully recover. They also benefit from a support system that can encourage them along the way in their own journey of healing. Therefore, if you feel this subject matter might be too intense for you, or you want to learn about it at another time, you can skip this last chapter and go on to the next book and continue the journey through the last pothole. If you want to continue, however, be assured that if it gets too intense, you can come away from the content at any time, connecting back with the Lord and His intended emotions for you.

It is always good to keep in mind that Jesus has given us the Holy Spirit to lead us into all truth. The Holy Spirit is our Comforter, our Companion, and our Guide. He is the One who will never leave or forsake us. Through these books, we have become equipped with the tools we need to delve deeper, so if there are any emotions that get stirred up, be assured they can be managed by using the emotional chart we studied, the 5 R's, and the new lessons learned about removing lies from our hearts. As we use the tools in our tool belts, we will stay safe and come away victorious.

Before taking on the challenges of the fractured heart, it is so important to first understand the basics of personalized wounds, because these basics help us heal our hearts when they are fractured. We discovered how to find the lies we believe and the remedy for these lies, and we now have the foundation necessary to understand how the fractured heart gets healed.

The Humpty Dumpty Heart

Even though we have used eggs as an analogy for lies, there is another analogy involving just one egg that is a very effective way to describe the subject of fracturing.

I'm wondering how many people still remember the famous old English nursery rhyme, "Humpty Dumpty." He was an egg-man with quite a tragic story about taking a deadly fall after being precariously perched on a wall. It reads like this:

Humpty Dumpty sat on a wall.

Humpty Dumpty had a great fall.

All the king's horses and all the king's men

Couldn't put Humpty together again.

Years ago, as I read that nursery rhyme to our very small children, I remembered it as a whimsical, harmless little poem I had learned as a child. So I playfully read it to them, until it hit me, and I realized what a horrible story it actually was. I was indignant as I thought of the millions of little innocent hearts over the centuries who heard of that poor little egg-man smashed all over the ground. Was he a hard-boiled egg or a soft-boiled one? Or worse yet, was he a raw egg? Any way he was cooked, it was innards and broken shell everywhere! How depressing and final—and hopeless! After all, if no one could fix him, he was a *DEAD* egg! As all these thoughts ran through my mind, I decided to make up my own ending to somehow redeem this ever-so-short preschool tale. It didn't rhyme, but it conveyed the message I wanted my children to know. It went something like this, *"...All the king's horses and all the king's men couldn't put Humpty together again. But Jesus knows how to fix everything, and nothing is impossible with Him, so He can put Humpty back together and make him just like new!"* It was not very poetic, but it brought redemption into an otherwise hopeless story. I realize I may have overreacted just a little to this four-line poem back then, but since that time I have worked with many brokenhearted people over the years, and I have seen the tremendous value of placing hope into the hearts of those who feel like they have experienced just what Humpty did.

Each of our hearts can be compared to an egg in this way. Just like our hearts, every egg is very soft and tender on the inside and has a fragile shell as a boundary, or border, that keeps everything in place. Our shells were never created to be like concrete, so hardened that nothing could destroy them. They were meant to be soft, pliable containers that fostered the potential of life within. At the right season, when all was properly formed inside, they were meant to give way, allowing the new life inside to emerge into all its glory.

But some eggs didn't get the treatment they needed; some were not as protected as they should have been. Some got bruised and battered or were even dropped. For those eggs, life didn't happen as it should have. They were often discarded as unusable.

Like eggs, our hearts can also be bruised, battered and break in similar fashion. Wounds inflicted upon our hearts vary in severity—from small hairline cracks to the deep, life-altering breaks, where our hearts shatter. I call hearts with these wounds the *Humpty Dumpty Hearts*. The title isn't meant to diminish or lighten the condition of these hearts; it is only meant to describe them in the simplest way possible. These are the wounds that are so severe, so dramatic and deep, that our hearts break apart completely into separate pieces. It was never God's design for our hearts to have to endure such trauma, but because of mankind's fallen nature and the dark, abusive choices of others, there are multitudes who have had to live through the pain of this extreme trauma.

Fracturing is one of the terms used to describe what happens to our hearts in times of excessive trauma or wounding. Just a few examples of such excessive wounding could include war, personal violence of any kind or the threat of violence to ourselves or those we love, long-term abuse, natural disasters, or sudden accidents. Like we read in the first chapter of this book, it can result in pieces of our hearts breaking off completely, creating a shattered and scattered heart instead of a whole one. Some people refer to this break as *dissociation*. When dissociation is severe, two of the names used for this condition are *Dissociative Identity Disorder (DID) or Multiple Personality Disorder (MPD)*. There is a wide spectrum of dissociation and we all do it to some degree. But it becomes problematic when it affects our ability to live in relationship with others in normal, healthy ways.

A Fractured Heart

The wide spectrum of fracturing can be daunting to understand. As I tried to wrap my own mind around the subject years ago, I found that I could most easily connect to it as I looked to the heart itself.

The individual chambers of the whole heart function together as one. The spirit picks up information from the world and sends this information to the soul for interpretation and to the body for expression, just like we learned in the first book of this series. As the four chambers work together, a continuous flow of information is taken in, interpreted and released back out through communication. There can be minor glitches in this process as we mature, but generally speaking, our heart works together as one complete unit to function in the world in which we live.

A fractured heart, I found, operates a bit differently. When a fracture occurs in the spiritual heart, each broken piece can create a personality of its own, and some would say, a heart of its own as well. These individual parts, or pieces of the heart do their best to help a person function in the duties and responsibilities of life, but it is clear that the lives they live are done in the context of surviving not thriving.

So how can we tell if our hearts have fractured? What does it feel like to have a fractured heart? To answer those questions, let's divide the subject of fracturing into two categories: Simple Fractures and Complex Fractures. Just like the bones of our body, the emotional injuries we sustain can be as slight as a crack or as severe as many breaks, depending upon the gravity of the damage done. It is much the same with our hearts.

Simple Fractures

We have all had times when we have tried to make a decision, only to discover that one part of our heart wants to do one thing and another part wants to do something totally different. We even say things like, *"Part of me wants to go enjoy myself at the movies today but part of me wants to stay home and finish the assignment I was given to do."* Those who function from a unified heart can process through the conflict and come to a conclusion relatively quickly without much internal disruption.

If, however, these conflicts tend to stalemate us and stop our ability to make decisions in order to move forward, it can be an indicator of a *simple fracture*. The Apostle Paul called it being *double-minded*. (6.1) Jesus said, *"If a house is divided against itself, that house will not be able to stand."* (6.2) We are the temple, or "house" of the Lord, (6.3) and if our hearts are divided by double-mindedness, they will not have the strength to stand when dealing with the pressures of life. Without healing we eventually fall, giving way to the eroding consequences of a divided heart.

So when we identify simple fractures in our hearts, such as double-mindedness, it is important to ask the

Holy Spirit some questions to resolve the conflicts within, such as:

- *Why do I want to do these two differing things?*

- *What is the root issue that is dividing my heart?*

- *Is my spirit hearing one thing but my soul saying another?*

- *Is it fear or some other negative emotion?*

- *Is it my will vs. God's will for me?*

- *Are all four chambers of my heart in sync?*

- *What is my intellect saying?*

- *What are my emotions saying?*

- *What is my spirit saying to me?*

- *What decision will bring my heart the most peace right now?*

These questions may take effort and focus, but if we take the time to get away from the pressure around us long enough to answer them, they will quickly take us into the deeper places of our hearts. The answers to the questions will help us discover the root of the problem or perhaps which pothole is causing the problem. Using the 5 R's to bring the remedy for the problem can unify the heart once again.

Complex Fractures

Feelings of internal chaos within may indicate more complex fracturing. Internal chaos can manifest itself as an inability to maintain inner peace and quiet. Instead of peace and quiet, a person with complex fracturing may experience continuous activity in the mind, hearing many voices within, multiple and simultaneous internal conversations, background noise, and disorder or confusion as the norm. Other indicators of complex fracturing are lapses in memory, being unable to account for chunks of time in a day or a week, having feelings of "disappearing" in certain circumstances, or an inability to connect emotionally with others, just to name a few.

In some cases there are fractures that present themselves as individual personalities—entities unto themselves—all within one person. These will manifest in distinct personas: a playful one, one who needs to maintain control, a funny and entertaining one, a rebellious one, a religious one, and so on. They may all be anonymous, or they may have individual names for each persona. In the past, some well-meaning people believed and treated these individual personalities as demonic spirits. So much has been learned in the last several decades, however, about fracturing that those with experience are able to distinguish between the personalities of a deeply fractured heart and a demonic spirit manifesting itself. The boundaries of this book series do not afford us the opportunity to explore this subject in depth, but there are numerous resources online for those who want more in-depth teaching or training on this subject.

In my own experience, I have observed individual personas all working together to create balance in a person's life, so a degree of internal stability can be maintained. When fracturing is complex, we must realize it is the heart working diligently to cope with the overwhelming circumstances of a life filled with trauma it was never designed to carry. Even in this type of severe fracturing, we see how intricately we were created. We were designed with such complex systems that, when necessary, we adapt in order to survive. Though this was never God's original plan for us, He put within us the ability to overcome and be victorious in even the harshest of conditions.

Healing the Fractured Heart

God's plan has always been for more than just survival—He longs for us to thrive. So whether the fractures of the heart are minimal or extreme, the answer for healing these deep inner breaks is the same as for those whose hearts are more intact. Each broken piece must come into a relationship with Jesus where we allow Him to take His rightful place as King of the heart. Then each piece must address the potholes they have individually fallen into by repenting, forgiving, renouncing and receiving the truth, as the Lord gives it.

When an individual participates in the redemptive work of healing the fractures of the heart, there is a supernatural component that takes place. At some point, whether it is right away or more slowly over time, the broken pieces come together into one whole person once again. Because each piece, or persona has its own heart, and therefore its own will, there is a decision that each one gets to make. The decision is whether to entrust their heart to Jesus. The fracture itself is a coping mechanism—a protection because of trauma. Therefore the part that broke off needs to trust Jesus to take care of the person it is protecting. Sometimes each of the personas gather together in unison and go to Jesus or even go *into* Jesus. The Bible says *"In Him we live and move and exist,"* [6.4] so it is a valid concept to have the pieces of the broken heart go *into Him* to find life and healing. Other times, it will be one broken piece at a time that becomes able to trust in Jesus' protection and be reconciled to the heart of God, integrating into the greater whole of the individual person. So whether a person's heart has a simple fracture, or has been broken into many pieces, every heart deserves to be brought to the One who can heal.

The journey is an intricate one at best, and every person is different. Just like our fingerprints, no two people are alike, so we need the Holy Spirit to guide and bring the necessary wisdom and power to accomplish healing. Jesus spoke the truth when He told His followers, "...*apart from Me, you can do nothing.*" (6.5) As we take Him at His word, we must trust that He, by way of His Spirit residing within, will be able to accomplish the work of healing the heart.

The process of allowing God to heal the heart can be likened to the picture seen by one of the prophets in the Bible. God took the prophet Ezekiel to a vast valley filled with dry, very old bones. Read the story below:

> *The LORD took hold of me, and I was carried*
> *away by the Spirit of the LORD to a valley filled*
> *with bones. He led me all around among the*
> *bones that covered the valley floor. They were*

scattered everywhere across the ground and were completely dried out.

Then He asked me, "Son of man, can these bones become living people again?" "O Sovereign LORD," I replied, "You alone know the answer to that." Then He said to me, "Speak a prophetic message to these bones and say, 'Dry bones, listen to the word of the LORD! This is what the Sovereign LORD says: Look! I am going to put breath into you and make you live again! I will put flesh and muscles on you and cover you with skin. I will put breath into you, and you will come to life. Then you will know that I am the LORD.'" So I spoke this message, just as He told me. Suddenly as I spoke, there was a rattling noise all across the valley. The bones of each body came together and attached themselves as complete skeletons. Then as I watched, muscles and flesh formed over the bones. Then skin formed to cover their bodies, but they still had no breath in them. Then He said to me, "Speak a prophetic message to the winds, son of man. Speak a prophetic message and say, 'This is what the Sovereign LORD says: Come, O breath, from the four winds! Breathe into these dead bodies so they may live again.'" So I spoke the message as He commanded me, and breath came into their bodies. They all came to life and stood up on their feet—a great army. Then He said to me, "Son of man, these bones represent the people of Israel. They are saying, 'We have become old, dry bones—all hope is gone. Our nation is finished.' Therefore, prophesy to them and say, 'This is what the Sovereign LORD says: O my people, I will open your graves of exile and cause you to rise again. Then I will bring you back to the land of Israel. When this happens, O my people, you will know that I am the LORD. I will put my Spirit in you, and you will live again and return home to your own land. Then you will know that I, the LORD, have spoken, and I have done what I said. Yes, the LORD has spoken!'" (6.6)

So it is with the fractured heart. The Lord was able to knit all the dry bones together and bring them to life once again, and He is also able to bring all the fractured pieces of the heart together again and make them completely whole and new. He is able to breathe His breath of life into each one, so they can live from a whole heart again. We know the One who is able to fix the broken parts that *"all the king's horses and all the king's men"* couldn't fix is also the One who can resurrect a heart that has been deeply broken. It is because of His great love for us that He reaches down from heaven and brings His supernatural superglue to make the brokenhearted whole. It is merely our job to trust Him to do so.

Summary

The purpose for addressing the fractured heart in this book series is primarily to shed light on the truth that some people's personalized wounds are not as simple to heal as they may appear at first glance.

Those who struggle with a lack of healing progress may have underlying conditions that must be considered. An example would be a person who visits a doctor for what appears to be a relatively minor symptom. The doctor listens to the presenting symptoms but looks beyond to find a broader, more significant underlying disease. If the doctor only treats the symptom, he will not heal the underlying disease.

The subject of fracturing is the underlying disease in *some* people's hearts, and if that is what they suffer from, they will need the aid of someone who can help the fractured heart find its healing.

It is also important to note that not everyone should be viewed as fractured. We must be careful not to swing too far in either direction. One extreme view is that fracturing doesn't exist or is only demonic in nature, while the opposite extreme view is that every person is fractured. Neither extreme is grounded in truth. As we press into the Lord for wisdom, we will be able to rightly assess each person as the individual God created him or her to be.

In closing this chapter I would like to offer one caution to those who minister inner healing to others:

I have seen significant damage done to people's hearts when healing hasn't come quickly. When prayer has not fixed the problem in one easy step, it is important to avoid attributing any slowness or lack of healing to unbelief or anything else that would impose shame or guilt on the person in need of the healing. Such things are the tools of the enemy and run counter to the love and compassion of Jesus, who is ultimately the one responsible to bring healing to the wounded heart.

<u>Conclusion</u>

We have covered a lot of territory in this book. We discovered the definition of the term Personalized Wounds by way of one of the parables Jesus told His followers. Then we explored the lies that those personalized wounds represent. We found out there are many types of lies we can believe, but all lies have one thing in common: they are lies because they do not align with the truths of heaven.

We also learned about the four categories of emotions. Each of these categories helps us to identify what is happening inside of our hearts. When we feel *God's Intended Emotions,* we know we are connected to the feelings God planned for us all along. With *Truth Based Emotions,* we understand the need to express, validate, and resolve the feelings that are the result of the fall. We do that as we pray and give those emotions to the Lord in order for healing to take place. When we experience *Vengeful Emotions,* we know we have partnered with the enemy and we must repent of our sinful partnership. Finally, we learned that *Satan's Opposing Emotions* are the clues that lead us to the lies that have been planted into our hearts. As we identify the lies and apply the remedy, we are set free to live from a place of truth and freedom once again. We also learned about two "tricky" emotions—anger and depression. Both are secondary emotions, meaning there are other primary emotions that exist underneath them. Anger can be righteous or unrighteous and can mask the sense of injustice our hearts carry. It can also mask the pain that comes from wounding. The roots of depression, on the other hand, are found in either deception or rebellion.

Finally we looked at the fractured heart and learned about the resiliency of the heart to cope with significant wounding. Whether trauma has caused simple or complex internal fractures, it is important for us to partner with the Holy Spirit to find the answers to bring our heart into the unity and oneness God designed it to have.

As we look forward to the 7th and last book of this series, we will be focusing on our final pothole—*Inherited Wounds*. These wounds are also on the deception side of the Detour Road, and we will find out why they are deceptive in nature. We will be discovering how those who have lived before us in our family lines have affected the degree to which we find ourselves able to live wholeheartedly. We learn how to honor those who have gone before us, even if they have not acted in ways that would be considered honorable, and we learn the skill of taking our ancestors before God's throne to partner with heaven and break the cycle of these inherited wounds.

When you are ready to conquer our final pothole, go to www.heartofheavenminitries.com to purchase the final book in this series *Living From a Whole Heart.*

End Notes

Chapter 1:

    1.1   Jeremiah 29:11

Chapter 2:

    2.1   Jeremiah 31:33

Chapter 3:

    3.1   Smith, Ed. D. Min. (2000). *Beyond Tolerable Recovery* (Chapter 4). Campbellsville, KY: Family Care Publishing.

    3.2   Friesen, James G. Ph.D., Wilder, James. Ph.D., Bierling, Anne. M.A., Koepcke, Rick. M.A., and Pool, Maribeth. M.A. (1999, 2000, 2004). *The Life Model: Living From the Heart Jesus Gave You* (Chapter 3). Pasadena, CA: Shepherd's House, Inc.

Chapter 4:

    4.1   John 10:4,5

    4.2   Matthew 7:7, 9-11

    4.3   Hebrews 3:7-8

    4.4   1 John 4:1

    4.5   Hebrews 11:6

    4.6   Luke 6:28; Romans 12:14; James 3:10

    4.7   Matthew 21:12-16; Mark 11:15-18; Luke 9:45-47

    4.8   Adams, Debbie. (2014). *Living From a Whole Heart: Wounding Others* (Chapter 1). Redding, CA. Heart of Heaven Ministries.

    4.9   Isaiah 54:14

    4.10   Genesis 4:4-7 (Amplified)
According to most Bible scholars, the reason

God did not accept Cain's offering of produce from the land was because God had already established the need for a blood sacrifice as an offering for sin (Gen 3:21). This type of sacrifice was a prophetic picture of Christ, who was to come, sacrificing His own blood on the cross to pay the penalty for sin. That is why Abel's offering was pleasing to God, while Cain's was insufficient. God gave Cain a way to redeem himself and the chance to choose the right thing to do. God also graciously gave Cain a warning, letting him know that sin was at his door, wanting to devour him. Ultimately God gave Cain the choice to do what was right, but Cain chose to act out his anger instead, murdering his brother. (Gen. 4:8)

About the Author

Debbie Adams has been in the ministry of healing hearts since 1999. Her training has included studies in multiple inner healing models such as Elijah House, Theophostic Prayer Ministry, Restoring the Foundations International, Plumbline Ministries, and SOZO Ministry to name just a few. But her most extensive training has come from the school of the Holy Spirit, as she has partnered with God in the trenches of her life, where He has faithfully taught her the lessons needed for healing first her own heart and then the hearts of those she counsels. She is a licensed pastor and has ministered as a pastoral counselor since moving to Redding, California in 2004. She has also taught many classes on healing the heart, including the workshop she developed entitled, "Choosing the Heart of Heaven." She presently works with people of all ages, doing pastoral ministry and faith-based counseling for individuals and couples.

Debbie has been married to her husband Mike since 1977 and they have three children: Jeff, his wife Te'Aira, and Janna. They are also the very enamored grandparents of two grandchildren and a very large and loving Rottweiler, appropriately named "Dude."

Debbie's *Living From a Whole Heart* series contains the following titles:

20675816R00065

Made in the USA
San Bernardino, CA
20 April 2015